LESSONS ON
MORALITY, INTEGRITY, LOYALTY
AND PUBLIC SERVICE
FROM THE LIFE OF
BETTY AMONGI

LESSONS ON
MORALITY, INTEGRITY, LOYALTY AND PUBLIC SERVICE
FROM THE LIFE OF BETTY AMONGI

TONY AKAKI

LESSONS ON MORALITY, INTEGRITY, LOYALTY AND PUBLIC SERVICE FROM THE LIFE OF BETTY AMONGI

iUniverse books may be ordered through booksellers or by contacting:

iUniverse
1663 Liberty Drive
Bloomington, IN 47403
www.iuniverse.com
844-349-9409

Because of the dynamic nature of the Internet, any web addresses or links contained in this book may have changed since publication and may no longer be valid. The views expressed in this work are solely those of the author and do not necessarily reflect the views of the publisher, and the publisher hereby disclaims any responsibility for them.

Any people depicted in stock imagery provided by Getty Images are models, and such images are being used for illustrative purposes only.
Certain stock imagery © Getty Images.

ISBN: 978-1-6632-1803-2 (sc)
ISBN: 978-1-6632-1804-9 (e)

Print information available on the last page.

iUniverse rev. date: 02/05/2021

To

Chairperson Land Probe Commission
Lady Justice Bamugemeire

and other members:

Robert Ssebunnya, the Senior Presidential Advisor on
Buganda Matters, Mary Oduka Ochan, a development
expert, Joyce Gunze Habaasa, a land Consultant, Rose
Nakayi, an advocate, Fredrick Ruhindi, a former Attorney
General, George Bagonza Tinkamanyire former LCV
Chairperson, Hoima district, Ebert Isaiah Busobozi
Byenkya, a lawyer, Olive Kazaarwe Mukwaya, a judicial
officer, Douglas Singiza and John Bosco Rujagaata Suuza.

A leader cannot put himself or herself in a position in which his or her personal interests conflict with his or her duties and responsibilities. A leader shall not participate in the deliberations of a public body or board or council or commission or committee of which he or she is a member at any meetings at which any matter in which he or she has personal interest is to be discussed.

The Leadership Code Act (Amendment) Act, 2017

13

Tony Akaki

Tony Akaki

25

35

36

37

45

Bibliography

Constitution of the Republic of Uganda, 1995

The Code of Conduct for Members of Parliament Rules of Procedure Parliament of Uganda

The Holy Bible

The Holy Koran

Leadership Code Act (Amendment) Act, 2017

www.ingramcontent.com/pod-product-compliance
Lightning Source LLC
Chambersburg PA
CBHW051418250726
48655CB00003B/1119